LORD *FIX* MY LIFE

Copyright © 2018 Michelle Limes

Published by Godzchild Publications
a division of Godzchild, Inc.
22 Halleck St., Newark, NJ 07104
www.godzchildproductions.net

Printed in the United States of America 2018 - 1st Edition

All rights reserved. Except as permitted under the U.S. Copyright Act of 1976, this publication shall not be broadcast, rewritten, distributed, or transmitted, electronically or copied, in any form, or stored in a database or retrieval system, without prior written permission from the author.

>Library of Congress Cataloging-in-Publications Data
>Lord Fix My Life/Michelle Limes
>
>ISBN   978-1-942705-50-5 (pbk.)
>
>1. Limes, Michelle 2. Inspirational 3. Purpose 4. Self-Help
>5. Ministry 6. Christianity 7. Spiritual 8. Religion

2018

*In Loving Memory to my father Aaron Lee Peterson and my grandmother Amazie Louise Meadows.
I love you.*

Rest In Peace

ACKNOWLEDGEments

I would like to thank my husband R. Sean Limes for allowing me to work on this project. You are amazing. Words cannot express my gratitude to you for always being there and always loving me. I don't know what I would do with out you. I thank God for you being a shoulder to lean on during times I wanted to give up.

I also would like to thank my mother, Rebecca Peterson. I thank you for your continued encouragement and support. You are always there pushing me to WIN.

I dedicate this book to my children Marcus, Ashlee, Aaron and my granddaughter Maya. I pray you all will continue to grow and mature in the Lord as you walk this journey called life. Stay true to who God has created you to be. Each of you has what it takes to succeed. I will always be here for each of you, for I love you endlessly. Go and be GREAT!

TABLE OF Contents

Foreword   *[i]*
Introduction *[v]*

Chapter 1.   *Acknowledgement [1]*

Chapter 2.   *Know the Power of Prayer and Faith [13]*

Chapter 3.   *Know the Power of Words [33]*

Chapter 4.   *Renew Your Mind [45]*

Chapter 5.   *Heal Me [59]*

Chapter 6.   *Know Your Enemy [75]*

Chapter 7.   *Eliminate The Baggage of Unforgiveness [91]*

Chapter 8.   *Find Your Happy Place! [105]*

Chapter 9.   *Clean Out Your Closet [115]*

About the Author   *[129]*

Have you ever been in a season where it seems as if nothing you do match up to your own expectations? Are you in a place where you feel unclear or uncertain about direction, meantime everything around you seems cluttered and you can't see your way through? Well, if that is you…. "Lord, Fix My Life" provides you with simple tools to help navigate through the land mines of life using the divine principals of the Word of God.

In each chapter Rev. Michelle Limes help you to dig deeper into identifying and understanding the root cause of some of the situations and occurrences that seem to repeat themselves. This book will give you the solutions on how to successfully move forward through life.

I've learned over the years, that change will only come if you are open to it and not afraid to orchestrate it. So, if you are serious about making a change, "Lord Fix My

Life" is the answer to many of your questions on how to break the cycle of self-destruction and begin to gain more self-awareness and confidence to not just FIGHT the battles but also WIN the wars in every area of your life.

Now, by the power of the Holy Spirit, I call forth clarity and understanding to help guide you to a place of self-awareness, peace and empowerment in Jesus name. Now, go get your life back!

God Bless You!

Dr. Zina Pierre
The Breaking Room
Author, Pastor and Political Strategist

Take a good look at the closet featured on the cover of this book. Now, think of this closet as a metaphor for the crazy parts of each of our lives. To make it personal, think of your own life, specifically. The mere fact that you are holding this book suggests one of two things. Either you were drawn by the cover and title and curious to see what it is about, or you desire to see a shift for changes to be made in your own life. If the latter applies to your situation, here is your warning: once you invite God to enter your life, be prepared to endure a thorough purging process. God works through process.

Back to your closet, you see all sorts of stuff. It is packed sky high from side to side. There are clothes balled up on the floor, along with, some stuff that simply does not belong. There is a tennis racket, a big ball, and all sorts of things that are taking up space. Space that should be reserved for what does belong. There is also a bag being smashed up because of the other things that are out of order in your closet.

While thinking about your life's closet, ask yourself the following questions: What do I need to get out of my closet? What is taking up space? What doesn't belong there? How do I organize this closet better? Do I need more hangers? What should be removed from my life's closet, so that good things can be added in their place? How do I put the pieces back together in my life that have been broken? How do I get my life back on track?

There will be a multistep process outlined in each chapter of this book along with scripture references that I have found to be helpful in my own life. I have also shared personal testimony and a few reflective exercises for application. As you read along, it is my prayer that you become more open to let God fix your life. You may become uncomfortable during the process, but don't throw this book down. Keep reading. Your happiness and your freedom depend on this. See the benefits that await you on the other side of *change* and move forward.

Acknowledgment

Whoever conceals their sins does not prosper, but the one who confesses and renounces them finds mercy. – Proverbs 28:13 NIV

Identify what is in your closet. This is the first step. It may be tempting to skip past this part of the process, but it would be to your detriment. The irony is we think we know what we have been holding onto, but the truth is we have no clue because we have been holding on for so long. We have packed so many things on top of each other that many unresolved issues have been buried underneath all the clutter within our hearts. Sometimes we shut the door on our closets, so we can pretend a little longer that our houses, which symbolize our total being, are clean. And, long as we keep the door closed, we can continue our existence under the false notion that all is well. No, all is not well, but there is hope. We will be able to properly confront our issues accordingly through our confession. I know it is no fun to air our dirty laundry, but in this situation, you are uncovering it for yourself and for God only. It is due time that we acknowledge the predicaments we are in, our feelings, and the habits that brought us to this undesirable place.

Let us face it, we all get comfortable sometimes. And when we find ourselves coasting along in the comfort zone, that is when we just casually toss things into our closets. We are taking no account for the things we are accumulating and before we know it, our closets become piled up with stuff that does not belong. There are layers of suppressed memories that were too painful for us to deal with in the past. Some, we have suppressed for so long, if anyone called us out on our issues, we would look at this individual as though he or she were crazy, and we would quickly denounce the observation. Thankfully, God has a *fix* for this. God can endow us with tools that will help us to effectively maintain our closet space. The truth of the matter is it will be uncomfortable to do this at times, but we can take joy in knowing God's Word which says, "…Never will I leave you; never will I forsake you" (Hebrews 13:5 NIV).

> *Let us face it, we all get comfortable sometimes.*

If you picked up this book, it suffices to say you desire to know the steps it takes to get past your anger and to move forward in your life. This chapter establishes the first step, *acknowledge*, and I am sure you may be thinking, "Okay, but acknowledge what?" I am so glad you asked. You must acknowledge the areas where you are struggling. While we live in a culture where people automate, "I'm fine," when they really are not, we will utilize an approach that is totally opposite from this notion throughout this book. No, you are not fine and that is okay. You are on the right track and God has always been right here waiting for you to call on Him for help.

    You can't confront what you won't confess. Acknowledge the source of your anger, hurt, pain, and unhappiness. Acknowledge the areas where you require discipline. Could it be stewardship? How are you with managing your finances? Do you tend to blow your budget and just spend frivolously, or, is self-control your issue? Do you move about haphazardly and just blow up on anyone who rubs you the wrong way on any given day? Is it always someone else's fault? Whenever things go wrong, do you typically shift the blame and point fingers? Have you ever accepted accountability for your own actions, partially and totally? What coping mechanisms have you developed over time? Are they good or bad?

    Are you accustomed to picking up a cigarette or what about marijuana or maybe you find pleasure in sedating yourself through popping pills? Do you like to go shopping when you are having a bad day? Perhaps, sex is your thing? Do you find yourself sleeping around with many partners so that you can avoid dealing with the pain of your past, childhood traumas, or poor decisions you made in your life? Maybe your unhappiness lies in some more recent decisions you have made? Have you attempted to practice discipline in all areas of your life? Are you able to exhibit portion control when eating food or are you an emotional eater? Do you over limit your food intake? No matter how good we strive to be, all human beings have our things that we need to deal with.

Do you struggle with a need for validation? It is time to acknowledge the pain you feel. For me, it was the rejection of my dad not being in my life. Perhaps, you can relate? Have you ever felt left behind or abandoned by anyone? Sometimes, because things don't look well in our lives, we can even feel abandoned by God, but this is simply not true. Once you complete the steps outlined in this book, you will come to know this for yourself. There is more good news, God desires to help you! Simply acknowledge these things so that you can readily ask God to replace these bad coping mechanisms with positive ones.

Acknowledgement is very important because your life's unresolved issues could be altering the way you respond to situations in general, and how you respond to the people you are involved with in close relationships. The unfortunate fact is when we have yet to acknowledge what's ailing us, not only do we tend to take it out on loved ones, but we also unleash unnecessary hurt on complete strangers if they happen to be around us at the wrong time. Yes, it is true: "hurt *people, hurt* people." You do not have to remain in the same place that you have dwelled for years any longer. God is ready to help you make this shift. You may be thinking, "It's too late for me. How can I possibly overcome after all I have done?" Just as sure as you can hear yourself saying this, also hear God saying, "Try Me."

> *Acknowledgement is very important because your life's unresolved issues could be altering the way you respond to situations in general, and how you respond to the people you are involved with in close relationships.*

Acknowledge your hurt. Acknowledge your pain. Acknowledge you need God. He is ready to take over and heal you, but He will only do so with your permission. God is truly compassionate, and some refer to Him as a gentleman. Considering this, He has provided us all with the option of choice. It is up to us. We get to choose. Life with Him or life without Him.

Before I began to see God operate within my own life, I had to face myself in the mirror. It was difficult. There were times when I did not want to look at what was in front of me, my reflection, because it would have required for me to face where I was at that moment in my life. It hurt, and it was hard, but it was so worth it. I know that this was one of the best decisions I have ever made in my life. I know the main reason why I have been placed on God's path for my destiny is because I finally took my head out of the sand and acknowledged myself to be where I was at the time.

Yes, there is a time and a place for reflecting on where you want to be, your goals, and aspirations; but this step can only be successful after you have fully acknowledged and assessed where you are currently. Acknowledge and move forward today. You will be better for it.

As it is with anything we do with God, there is beauty in the notion that, not only will our acknowledgment help us, but it will also help those around us. Just imagine, first you will learn to love God. Then, you will understand how to better love yourself. This will come through knowing that you are enough exactly the way God made you. Then, you can successfully love your neighbor and work towards living in peace and harmony with others as God intended. Do not believe

> *Before I began to see God operate within my own life, I had to face myself in the mirror. It was difficult.*

the lie that this process is intended to beat you down further, instead embrace the notion that this process was designed to set you free!

Complete the exercise below to apply what you have been reading so far:

1) Acknowledge three areas where you are struggling in your life currently. Write them down. Commit to working through these specific issues as you read this book.

_____

_____

_____

_____

_____

_____

_____

_____

2) Identify the root cause for the areas of tension you are currently enduring. Write them down. These are the areas that you will need to resolve before tackling any surface issues, such as what you wrote down on item one.

_____

_____

_____

_____

_____

_____

_____

_____

_____

_____

_____

3) We are beginning with addressing three issues so that you might find early success and not become overwhelmed during the process. If for some reason your issues feel heavier than you anticipated, you may want to focus on addressing one at a time. Once complete, repeat the process by assessing another area that you desire to change for your personal well-being.

Know the Power of Prayer and Faith

> *If you remain in me and my words remain in you, ask whatever you wish, and it will be done for you. – John 15:7 NIV*

Now it is time to establish a plan to clean your closet. If you have ever attempted any cumbersome task without first, establishing a plan, then you know how chaotic the process can be. Knowing this, let us start this process differently. To effectively plan as Believers, we must invite God into the process. We do so through prayer and faith.

Prayer is so important! Faith is just as important. Prayer and faith go hand in hand. If we want God to fix our lives, we must be in a position of prayer. We must also have faith to believe that God will help us, no matter how severe our situations may be. Prayer is a spiritual communion with God as in

> *If we want God to fix our lives, we must be in a position of prayer. We must also have faith to believe that God will help us, no matter how severe our situations may be.*

supplication, thanksgiving, adoration, or confession. You must position yourself at God's feet in prayer – which simply means, go humbly to God, knowing that He is your Savior. Go to God trusting and believing that God wants what is best for you. The song writer says, "Don't pray and worry or worry and pray." We can't do both. God has shown me just how powerful prayer is through the manifestation of things I prayed for in the past. Because I, first, believed; now I see.

The Bible says, "Rejoice always, pray continually, give thanks in all circumstances for God's will for you in Christ Jesus," (1 Thess 5:16-18 NIV). We must pray without ceasing and pray God's will for our lives. We look at other people's lives and feel that we should have what they have. Sometimes we envy other people's relationships and status. Instead we should get in a position of prayer and say, "God, what do You want for my life? What have you designed my hands to do? Why am I here? What is my purpose?" We should ask God these things in prayer and He will reveal the answer in His time.

> *"God, what do You want for my life? What have you designed my hands to do? Why am I here? What is my purpose?"*

If prayer is new to you, it may seem strange speaking to a God that you cannot visibly see and, at first, you may believe that you cannot hear

God talk back to you. After pursuing God more, you will begin to discern the sound of His voice and know when He begins to speak to you in your heart. As we begin to listen when God speaks to our hearts, we find ourselves growing in Him. The more we listen and follow through with what God speaks, the more we grow in our attitudes, actions, thinking, and speaking. The Bibles says in Ezekiel 36:26a "And I will give you a new heart, and a new spirit I will put within you."

No matter what you've done or where you've been God loves you and still hears your prayers. Believe it! Make sure that you remain in a position of prayer and believe God at His Word, and discover what the will of God is for your own life. Ask God and seek God in all things. This is how you develop a lifestyle of prayer.

PUT YOUR PRAYER BOX ON GOD'S ALTAR

I have an altar in my home for prayer. Others have prayer rooms, which is a similar concept. On my altar, I have a prayer box. I have written prayers for years and I am always amazed when I look back and realize that God has answered every one of them. Reserve a dedicated space for prayer in your home and place your prayer box there. Choose a peaceful, isolated area. Write down those things that you want God to do in your life in faith.

I guarantee, you will see them come to pass. The Bible says, "Write the vision and make it plain" (Habakkuk 2:2). As you begin to write prayers, you will gain the perseverance to run towards your destiny.

Praying and waiting go hand and hand. God listens, and He answers at the right time according to His will. We must remember the Word of God, *"though it tarries, wait on it* (Habakkuk 2:3). Answers to our prayers may not come in the timeframe that we want, but we are to trust God while waiting. Listen, the wait is not always easy or comfortable. When we are sick and visit the doctor, the first thing we're asked is what brought us in that day and we tell the doctor our issue. This works in the same way with God. During the wait, we should ask God, "What is my next step, Which way should I go ?" These are prayers. We are supposed to expose and acknowledge our issues and tell God how we really feel. We often go to God in prayer and only tell Him the BIG STUFF that we consider to be important. God wants to hear about the little things too and the other things that we may falsely consider to be unimportant to Him, as well.

Though He is an all-knowing God, we form our relationships with God through prayer. The Bible says in Proverbs 3:6, "Acknowledge Him in all of your ways and He will direct your paths." Get free and get comfortable with God. Tell Him your secrets and deepest hurts. When we don't talk to God, we are internalizing those thoughts and it spreads like cancer. Then, we find ourselves harboring things that we never let go of formerly. Anytime something or someone stirs those feelings, wounds open back up and we get hurt and offended all over again. The healing process can never come about this way. We must, first, release, all our negative feelings to God such as: bitterness, unforgiveness, rejections, betrayal and so forth. We don't necessarily come to this overnight because as I said before, God works through process.

It took me a long time to get to this point because there was a time when I only talked to God about my wants. Yes, God wants to hear our desires, but He wants to hear those other things that we don't like to talk about also. Such as, how we've been hurt or not able to forgive. It is okay to say, "God, help me forgive." Pray and allow your belief in God to be strong. Before you know it, manifestation will take place in your life. God operates this way. We're operating beneath an open heaven - if we talk to the Lord and tell Him what our problem is and what our needs are, He answers. Make good use of your prayer box. And once it's full, lay it on the altar – as many times as needed, over and, over again.

BE PREPARED TO STRENGTHEN YOUR SPIRITUAL MUSCLES AS YOU BEGIN TO EXERCISE PRAYER MORE IN YOUR LIFE

There have been periods when I had to learn how to exercise more prayer in my life. One of those times was when my husband and I first got married. We experienced so much spiritual warfare. Both our mothers became ill within a short time frame of each other, amidst other trials. There are moments where we all are required to face many trials simultaneously. During my season of trials, I felt like I was constantly on my face before the Lord in prayer. Whatever storms you are facing or whatever your situation may be, pray; and God will fix it.

I had cancer in the past, and there was nothing that I could physically do to change that diagnosis. Thankfully, prayer can change all. Get excited about your future with God! No, there is nothing you can do to change the past, nor should you try to change it. "And we know that in all things God works for the good of those who love him, who[a] have been called according to his purpose" (Romans 8:28 NIV). Yes, God can use all the muck and grime that you've gone through for your good! Keep praying and trust that God hears your prayers. Know that God is repositioning you for a better future. Pray to God for help with changing your mindset.

It can be difficult to understand the purpose of enduring various trials, while you are going through them. James 1:1-4 tells us "Consider it pure joy, my brothers and sisters whenever you face trials of many kinds, because you know that the testing of your faith produces perseverance. Let perseverance finish its work so that you may be mature and complete, not lacking anything." This lets us know that there is purpose in every situation we go through. God uses these experiences to develop us for our next level in Him.

During our weakest times it can be hard to pray, but we must push. For it is during these times, that we remind ourselves that God does not require fancy or eloquent prayers. God just wants a few words we can utter from our hearts. That's all He is seeking from us. Romans 8:26 says "Likewise the Spirit helps us in our weakness. For we do not know what to pray for as we ought, but the Spirit himself intercedes for us with groanings too deep for words." This lets us know there will be times when we lack the strength to pray for ourselves, but the Spirit knows exactly what to pray for.

As pastors and intercessors, we often are called to pray for someone; anoint them, lay hands, even prophesy, and then, witness manifestation in his or her life. Afterwards while enduring our own hardships, our natural self asks, "Lord, You used me for them, but what about me? What's going to happen for me?" I consider this the sacrifice of service unto God.

Have Faith, Don't Worry, God is in Control

Philippians 4:6 reads, "Do not be anxious about anything, but in every situation, by prayer and petition, with thanksgiving, present your requests to God." Prayer has a sister; her name is Faith. You must believe God is going to do what He promised, and you do so by faith. *Faith is the substance of things hoped for and the evidence of things not seen* (Hebrews 11:1). Through faith, you must believe. There's no point in praying if you have no faith. Faith comes from developing a relationship with God and watching God's hand at work in your own life, as well as, others.

Faith in Marriage and Singlehood

It took faith for me to believe that God would send me a good husband after enduring two failed marriages. Because of them, I had reached a point of low self-esteem and depression. I began to worry about my life. I knew I desired marriage but was not sure if I could ever trust again or even love again. I had to learn that I had to put all my trust in God and not rush my process of healing.

Psalm 27:14 says, "Wait on the Lord: be of good courage, and he shall strengthen thine heart." I learned how to live this scripture and it taught me. Waiting is a good thing. When single, you learn about yourself. You can be *found* while waiting. What does this mean? The bible tells us that "He that finds a wife finds a good thing" (Proverbs 18:22), and I often say, "She that finds a husband, finds anything." We are often in love with being in love; allowing our desires to override our discernment. Some of us, are scared to be alone and we say to ourselves, "My clock is ticking, I need to get married soon." Don't put unnecessary pressure on yourself in a race against your biological clock. Don't you realize that God loves you so much that He will place you in a season of "waiting" to process and heal you in preparation for the mate He has for you? There is a blessing in waiting, so don't jump into another relationship to be fulfilled because it provides a false sense of fulfillment. We look for men and women to fill voids that only God can fill. Only God can show you who you are. Only God can validate you. Only God can love you like no one else. Know this, singleness is a gift and marriage is a gift as well, but we must have enough faith in God to follow His timing for our lives. If you are single, know that God keeps His promises. If the Holy Spirit has revealed marriage to you for your future, it will come to pass! If you are married know that your prayer life and faith in God is essential. Married couples must keep Christ first, always communicate, and keep your commitment to your covenant. After all, marriage symbolizes Christ's love for the church.

Faith and Trusting God's Timing

Many times, we desire things and we want to do them now, now, now. We should instead, exercise our faith, talk to the Lord and say, "God is it now time for me to do this? Do You need to do some other things first in my life? Do You need to make changes within me?" You do not want God to make changes within you when your spirit is not prepared to receive them. Your character will not change, if your spirit is not ready. Belief in God's process, results from spiritual alignment with God, and there's good news! God always makes sure we're ready. As you move forward in your faith with God, you will also begin to progress, grow, and love more. Your faith will begin to show that you agree, "Love covers a multitude of sin" (1 Peter 4:8). In accordance with your faith, God will begin to speak to you more.

It took faith in God to get out of my bad relationships and to believe that I would have a good marriage one day. It took faith to sustain me while I waited. In faith, I believed God to supply all my needs as a single parent and to supply the grace for me to be a good example and raise my son. In faith, I spoke that, "My life has to become better because I'm done with the poor decisions I made in the past." From that point onward, God began to open doors for me.

I attended church for years until I met my husband that God chose just for me, but it was in the wait that God gave me my reward. We've now been married 15 years! During the wait I had to speak over my life and at that time, I decided I would not compromise my new values. It took faith to do these things. Waiting was not always easy, but I made up my mind to wait on God and it was worth it. God built up my self-esteem while I waited. This was necessary so that I could be whole before uniting with my husband. It takes two whole people to join with God in a beautiful marriage. In case you're wondering, I met my husband while he was my son's mentor at church. What a wonderful way for God to allow me to see my husband's heart at work!

Our faith began to be tested in other areas after finding our happily ever after. Remember that season of trials I mentioned. During that period, we lost our home and a couple weeks later, we had to give up our car. We were still newlyweds who should have been floating on Cloud 9. It took a lot of faith and prayer to endure those trials. I had to pray more than ever and develop more faith in God to grow spiritually.

PROCESS & DEVELOPMENT

I believe God allows things to happen in our lives because of something I call process and development. Process and development are necessary for our faith. If it had not been for the tribulations, my faith might not have grown to be where it is today. So, I encourage you to boast in your weaknesses, trials included, as the Word of God says in 2 Corinthians 12:9! I have no regrets at all. I've been through so much, and regret nothing because everything I have gone through was purposeful. It was all necessary for the process and development of my faith. Even the stuff that I went through before I was saved. It was all purposeful because I can relate to a drunk, weed smoker, and a fornicator due to my past. Anything God does has a domino effect. When God does something, it's just like when one domino hits another and so on. God can do one thing and it can affect many. The many it does affect, will be affected differently, according to their needs. Process and development initiates at the beginning of your faith. Willingly allow God to take you through His process so that you might be developed further today!

According to the Bible, Jesus performed many miracles, signs and wonders, and just before Jesus healed anybody while He was on earth, He asked them a specific question. "Do you believe?" When they said "yes," many honestly thought the *touch* or *the Word* healed them, but what really healed

> *Process and development are necessary for our faith.*

them was their faith. It's the same way today. If you believe God and have faith, you can see manifestations of God. I tell people all the time who constantly run to different prophets, "That's great!" and I don't doubt prophets because I have the gift of prophecy myself. You can get prophesied to all day long, but if you're not willing to activate your faith in obedience to follow God's instructions and see that manifestation, you've missed God. For us to really know the will of God for our lives, we must be mindful that we do not allow our desires to override our discernment, and faith in God can help us to accomplish this.

Faith requires that we step outside our own expectations so that we can believe God has thought of the best way to turn our circumstance. I had to do this. The way God did it was not the way I thought He would. God had to show me, and He allowed all that I went through to happen, so I could see what was on the inside of me. It changed my life, it really did! The entire journey that God put me through has impacted me greatly. All of it! "It was good that I was afflicted because now I can follow Your statutes" (Psalm 119:71). Yes, it took these afflictions for me to see me. To understand the person God had created. For me to understand my weaknesses and strengths and the other things I needed to work on. And this self-examination, required strong

> *For us to really know the will of God for our lives, we must be mindful that we do not allow our desires to override our discernment, and faith in God can help us to accomplish this.*

faith in God.

Timing is so important to God! His Word says *"My ways are nothing like yours. Your ways are nothing like Mine"* (Isaiah 55:8-9). You must remember what you've been through. Remember where you've been, so when you meet that young girl or young man that's going through the same thing you survived, talk to her or him in faith, and say, "Listen, this is how I did it." Hopefully if she or he is willing, you can show through the Word of God how your faith has allowed you to reach a particular place in life.

Self-realization and self-actualization with strong faith in God requires more self-reflection. Reflect on the following questions and statements: "What are the things I want to have changed in my life by next year? I don't want to be the same person that I am now. I want to have progressed and advanced. I want to have done something different in my life. I want to have developed in a wonderful way." God is saying, "Yes, progress." Continue onward and ask yourself, "What dreams are dormant in me because I tried one time and failed?" Maybe you tried at the wrong time. God says, "My timing is not like yours." And while God does not exist within time, He placed our lives within time and our timing is very important to God. We must be in God's perfect timing. It does not mean our ideas are not going to work. Maybe the approach was wrong. Maybe the person you connected with was wrong. Maybe the timing was wrong. The Bible says, "Some things only come through fasting and praying." Turn your plate down and say, "God, what wrong have I done that I can correct right now? Continue to pray and have faith. Operate in a lifestyle of prayer and faith daily and do all you can for God's Kingdom by the authority God has granted to you through Jesus Christ.

Complete the exercise below to apply what you have been reading so far:

1) If you do not currently have a prayer life, set a goal to pray at least once daily for one week and invite God to speak to you. If you do have a prayer life, begin to exercise prayer more and strengthen your spiritual muscles to a new level.

_____

_____

_____

_____

_____

_____

_____

_____

2) If you do not have a prayer box, purchase, select, or create one this week.

3) Write down three prayers to place into your prayer box this week. And remember, God wants to hear about the BIG and small things in your life!

_____

_____

_____

_____

_____

_____

_____

_____

_____

_____

4) Recall the foundation of your thoughts on faith and figure out how this foundation has impacted your faith in God today. Write this down in a prayer journal.

5) Pray and ask God to eliminate anything that is a hindrance to your faith growing in Him daily.

6) What are some ways that you can promote further processing and development of your faith?

_____

_____

_____

_____

_____

_____

_____

Know the Power of Words

> *The tongue has the power of life and death,*
> *and those who love it will eat its fruit.*
> *– Proverbs 18:21 NIV*

It is time to act. Execute the plan that you established to clean your closet and give it the overhaul it so desperately needs! Encourage yourself. Speak through your fatigue, your doubts about your abilities, and move. Once you see the finished product and experience the freshness that will exude from your newly cleaned closet, you will know it was more than worth it. As a matter of fact, you will see it was essential to your progression.

Your Words Can Shape Your Life

You need to commit to the process for God to fix your life. The next step of that process is to learn the power that comes from the words spoken by your tongue (Proverbs 18:21); for not only does "the mouth speak what the heart is full of" (Luke 6:45 NIV), but everything that we visibly see was first spoken - good and bad. If you were to take the time and survey your own life, you could visibly trace the original words of things that have manifested into your reality. Some things are spoken repeatedly within our family units and passed down for generations, so it is very important that we pay attention and end the cycle of repeating words that produce bad fruit.

Yes, we have been subjected to a lot of garbage in the past that has become embedded within our minds. This trash eventually manifests in our speech, and what we say out of our mouths is based on what we've always heard. These seeds are planted in many of our lives during what I refer to as, *the foundational years*. During these critical years, we begin to learn practices that continue onward until the cycle is interrupted.

Many Believers say, "We are new creatures in Christ" (2 Corinthians 5:17), when first developing a relationship with God; but often, our language says the exact opposite: "I'm not smart enough." "I don't know how." "I will never get married." "I will never have children." "I will not finish school," and "I will not get the job I want." Revelation 21:5 NIV says, "He who was seated on the throne said, 'I am making everything new!' Then he said, 'Write this down, for these words are trustworthy and true.'" If your language does not correlate with the *newness* God has granted, begin speaking words that will yield what you desire to see manifest in your life with power and authority, today!

The Bible talks about *speaking things that are not as though they are* (Romans 4:17). We must learn to talk right. If a person keeps telling a lie, they are going to start believing it. If you keep saying the same old lie, eventually, your mind, your heart, and everything about you is going to believe that lie. If we start speaking life into situations that we feel are dead, God's power can resurrect those things. Out of your mouth comes words and your life follows your words' directives. If you keep speaking negative words over your life, negativity will show up. The opposite applies as well. We can begin to see our lives change when we speak positively and incorporate the Word of God.

YES, GOD CAN TOTALLY FIX YOUR LIFE! WILL YOU LET HIM?

When I started to learn the Word of God, I started thinking differently about myself. I started thinking differently about what I can do. I realized I can do all things through Christ. I had to condition myself to learn to speak differently, to speak life! We are the direct products of what we say out of our mouths. The beginning of letting God fix your life is changing your language. A lot of times we say things like, "I'm broke." Well, how can you be broke when you serve a God who is a Provider? How can you be broke and there is a check on the way? The doctor might have said, "you are sick," so you keep speaking in the atmosphere, "I'm sick." What you should be speaking instead is, "I'm healed regardless of what my diagnosis is or what the doctor says." The Bible asks an important question, 'Whose report will you believe?' (Isaiah 53:1). I don't know about you, but I'm going to believe the report of the Lord! Speak, what's not as though it is. Declare, "I'm healed." It is my belief that before God can fix our lives, we must first start speaking things into existence. We must begin to speak from our mouths what God has revealed to our hearts. Even though, we may not see it physically with our own eyes in the moment, we must trust that God is faithful to keep His promises.

YOU HAVE THE POWER TO SPEAK LIFE INTO THOSE YOU LOVE

Pastor Limes and I have counseled married couples and one situation comes to mind. The husband desired to receive more encouragement from his wife. I shared, "In the same way that horses are stroked with brushes to encourage them to keep racing, we should stroke our husbands' egos. We should be their biggest cheerleaders! Even though you might not see certain things in your husband today, you must speak what you know your husband has the potential to be over his life." Just as we must encourage ourselves, we must also encourage those we love by speaking life into them. David *encouraged himself* (1 Sam 30:6). It is necessary for our growth and well-being that we encourage ourselves, along with others.

God's Word demonstrates that if we live our lives upright before Him, He will give us the desires of our hearts (Psalm 37:4). We must realize that God wants us to win! God does not want us to be unhappy – He desires for us to be happy in Him. He does not want us to be lonely – He wants us to know He is a company keeper. We do not need to look for love in all the wrong places because God is love. Low self-esteem does not have to be our portion when He tells us who we are in His Word. We are "fearfully and wonderfully made" (Psalm 139:14a).

> *Speaking these things are especially important when the circumstances in front of you don't look like what you desire for them to be.*

Tell your inner self that "God wants the best for me." Speaking these things are especially important when the circumstances in front of you don't look like what you desire for them to be. Once you begin to speak your specific desires for your life, they will come to pass. It's just like when a person speaks a lie into the atmosphere, they start believing and their heart starts receiving those lies. God's *fix* will totally interrupt that process. It is important for you to start speaking things you know God has promised to you because God does not lie, and God does not mock us.

Isaiah 55:11 (NIV) reads, "so is my word that goes out from my mouth: It will not return to me empty, but will accomplish what I desire and achieve the purpose for which I sent it." God left it up to us to believe, and unfortunately, sometimes we put God in a box - despite our awareness of this scripture. Furthermore, God said He will bless you greater than anything you can ask, think or imagine (Ephesians 3:20-21). This lets us know that our minds can't fully fathom all the power God harnesses and desires to maneuver within our lives.

I have seen the principle of speaking things into existence

at work many times in my own life. There is a noteworthy example where I witnessed myself transition from speaking negatively to positively. Overtime fruitful words began to flow from me and I saw visible changes manifest accordingly. My family was disappointed in me for having my son out of wedlock. They decided I needed to get married. My family planned this big wedding and I wasn't ready to get married, neither was my son's father. This marriage became toxic, and after a while, we both agreed to part ways. I believe this is how it happens for many of us. I wasn't saved. I did not have a relationship with God. I got tired and after a while I started to change my mindset because I wanted better for myself. I always tell people when ministering about toxic relationships, "You're going to keep dealing with that until you're tired. When you are tired, then you will change. When you reach the end of yourself, you will have exhausted every resource you thought would work." I began to speak positivity into my own life. Before I could speak differently, I first, had to think differently. I began to say to myself, "I can do better." You, too, can do the same in your own life.

    Whatever your specific circumstance is, begin to speak life into it today! When we clean out our closets we sort the things we want to keep separately from the trash. God wants us to eliminate that trash. One example that I give when

> *God wants us to eliminate that trash.*

preaching is, "If I came to your door and said, 'Would you mind if I dump my trash in your backyard?' Of course, you would say, 'No.' And if I responded, 'Okay, no problem.' Then, Monday, I come and put a cup in your backyard and Tuesday, I put a plate. Wednesday, I put some napkins and Thursday, I put some trash bags. Friday, I put some more plates, Saturday, I put some more cups, and by Sunday, I will have dumped all my trash in your backyard, but I did it the way the enemy does, very subtly. When we know God, the enemy doesn't dump his trash all at once. The enemy is subtle, he does one thing at a time. Before you know it, you're deep in it."

If you begin to apply the knowledge you have received about the power of your own tongue and how your words shape your life, you will never view words the same ever again. No longer speak words that permit the enemy to gradually dump his trash in your yard. Before you know it, he'll try to enter every aspect of your life by filling your home with trash, if you do not operate in the authority that God has given you. Clean house today! What's in your closet?

Complete the exercise below to apply what you have been reading so far:

1) Identify statements that you have been rehearsing in your mind, and even out loud, that go against who you desire to be and who God created you to be. DO NOT WRITE THEM DOWN. Determine the opposite and turn these statements into positives for your life and write them down.

_____

_____

_____

_____

_____

_____

_____

_____

2) Perform this same exercise for the people you love and need to encourage.

_____

_____

_____

_____

_____

_____

_____

_____

_____

_____

3) Hang these positive statements in a location where you can see them daily. For some, a bathroom mirror is a great location!

CHAPTER Four

Renew Your Mind

> *That, however, is not the way of life you learned when you heard about Christ and were taught in him in accordance with the truth that is in Jesus. You were taught, with regard to your former way of life, to put off your old self, which is being corrupted by its deceitful desires; to be made new in the attitude of your minds; and to put on the new self, created to be like God in true righteousness and holiness.*
> *– Ephesians 4:20-24 NIV*

Resist the temptation to believe a cluttered closet works for you. Change your mind and you will begin to see a new system of organization unfold before your very eyes. With a renewed mind, you will purge what is necessary from your wardrobe and walk through your closet freely without stumbling over old junk.

God allows us to go through a necessary wilderness season at times, so that we can be purified and pruned of the old habits that need to die. The wilderness can come with its own set of tribulation and once you survive it, it is important for you

> *Ultimately the wilderness is designed to change your old mind into a new one.*

to allow God to show you the purpose of this season.

Ultimately the wilderness is designed to change your old mind into a new one. If we enter the wilderness holding onto our previous mindsets from our time of turmoil, we're setting ourselves up to die spiritually or become stuck. When we go through the wilderness asking for God to endow us with His mindset, His viewpoint, and His perspective; We are better able to try to keep our focus where God is. Own your thoughts. You thought them. Once you accept this notion, mind renewal can take place. If you accept responsibility for your thoughts and actions, you will be better able to combat the enemy.

We can become successful by eliminating a *fleshy* perspective and replacing it with the Spirit of God. The Bible says, "As he thinks in his heart, so is he" (Proverbs 23:7). Yes, your thoughts control your life and what has manifested in front of you is the result of what you thought yesterday. Proverbs 4:23 (NLT) instructs you to "Guard your heart above all else, for it determines the course of your life." What we see, hear, and experience becomes content we meditate on. This exposure can eventually impact our thoughts and actions and imprint a specific way of thinking in our minds. Thanks be to God for giving us all the power to change the condition of our lives. If you are not living well, change your mind, and when you change your mind, you will change your life!

I came to realize a key ingredient for my change was allowing the Lord to purge me of the defense mechanism I had built up for years that stood like a giant wall. This wall protected my old way of thinking. The Bible says, "Create within me a pure heart so I won't sin against You" (Psalm 119:11). I said this often because it was my desire for God to cover my life in this way. I was stuck. Sometimes our minds get locked into systems of thinking, feelings, and emotions that prevent us from moving forward. This usually happens when we have been set in our ways, doing something wrong that we thought was right. Often the real reason we are stuck is because God is prompting us to eliminate the old patterns of thinking we picked up in the past that are hindering us presently.

I Am a Victor Not a Victim

We have all experienced downturns in our lives. These events can range from losing a job, becoming ill, to losing a loved one. It fascinates me that individual people can react differently to the same set of circumstances. We all possess the power to move according to God's will when presented with good or bad with the Holy Spirit as our guide. Contrarily, when we operate in a victim mindset, we essentially give our power away. We are exiting the place of powerlessness and no control and it can be a difficult transition to make. Meanwhile, we operate in pity parties and consistently blame and complain about our circumstances and we are frequently defensive as a result. Anything that is said to us and rubs us the wrong way, we take it personal because we are wearing our feelings on our sleeves. Unbeknownst to us, we are playing the role of victim.

I had to decide that I am not a victim but a victor, for every trial we endure there is something we may learn. From enduring various financial trials, such as when my son and I found ourselves homeless, I learned how to be a better financial steward over my resources. For every medical attack I have endured, I was able to witness and experience for myself that our God is a healer. Because of these things and more, I can say to you: Don't allow past trauma to leave you with a victim mindset.

When you choose to be a victor, you will feel empowered. Refuse to let your situation get the best of you. When something happens that you do not like, do not blame others, but accept personal responsibility. Maintain a positive attitude about your life and be positive in general when things don't go as you expect. This will help you feel in control of your personal well-being and will give you an assurance that everything will be alright. As victor, you will begin to feel good about yourself and will become more proactive.

Letting go is essential to embracing your victor mindset.

LET GO

Letting go is essential to embracing your victor mindset. Whatever happened that traumatized you or hurt you and caused pain in your life; can tempt you to continue the role of victim. We must renew our minds, so we can let things go. We must view what we went through differently because we're still here, and this proves that God still has purpose for our lives. If it did not kill us, God can still use us. Even if while enduring the process of what we went through, we felt we were on our last leg. Even if we spent a long time being in the valley, where we couldn't see the light at the end of the tunnel, and we didn't know how God was going to work it out. We are still here for some reason and we are still surviving. We are still operating in our day to day functions and we can still pray. We can still read God's Word. That lets you know you have the victory!

This is how you know that you are not a victim because God begins to show you that your pain has purpose and your past is useful for what God is building in your present and future. Romans 8:28 (NIV) says, "And we know that in all things God works for the good of those who love him, who[a] have been called according to his purpose." Commit this scripture to memory and allow God to write it on your heart. I cannot say this enough, renew your mind and you will change your life. You are not a victim. You are a victor!

Yes, great tragedy has happened. You may have been molested. You may have been raped and those are all bad things! However, you are still here. You are still here. Let's pause for a moment and take that in. You've got more life in you. You've got more fight in you and God wants to use your life to do some glorious things, if you will only let Him.

Now, see how God is going to work those trials in your life so that you will be free from the ongoing torment of the enemy replaying the assault and the attacks in your mind. Don't allow Satan to torment you anymore. No longer believe the lie that it is your fault or that you did something to cause the things that you have gone through.

> *No longer believe the lie that it is your fault or that you did something to cause the things that you have gone through.*

Remember it is all about changing your perspective. You are shifting from victim to victor. It's all about perception. How you perceive what you went through, is essential to how you will live out the remainder of your days on earth. If you view your past from a, "I'm doomed" perspective, you cannot go further.

If you view God as in control of all things, despite your bad experiences, then you will believe God will make it work for your good. Understand God does not will harm for your life, but we live in a fallen world where evil attacks persist. After processing the grief of what has hurt you, ask God to show you how He is turning it around on your behalf. Say, "I'm hurting so God I need You to help me with this hurt. Please put Your love on my wounds to heal me. My wounds are still open. I haven't dealt with my wounds and they still bother me." There are many times when we're in pain, when we are hurt, when we are dealing with things and we seek aid from other people. We seek pastors, we seek bishops, we seek ministers, we seek mama, we seek daddy, we seek grandma and God is saying, "No, I don't want you to put your trust in any man or woman. I want you to lean on Me and know that I'm the only one that can heal you completely." Put on your new mindset and pursue God with all your being.

Yes, God does raise up people in our lives to help us

go through the process of letting go, but we must know the ultimate source of our healing comes from God. Even if God does uses someone else, He is the source. Remember, we must revisit our pain, so we may be propelled to a place of victory. This is especially true when transitioning from victim to victor. Sometimes you must go back to go forward. And when we go back, we don't wallow in it, but we do need to confront our past hurts exactly where they are. Resist temptation from the enemy to slip it all under the rug. Invite God in, submit to His will for your life so that He can accelerate your path for manifestation. Release the lies that the enemy has told you. Now it is your time to come out and you will, if you allow God to renew your mind and you employ His wisdom for your life.

Complete the exercise below to apply what you have been reading so far:

1. How have the previous difficult seasons you endured proven themselves as being purposeful in your life? How has your level of discernment been developed? How has your strength increased?

_____

_____

_____

_____

_____

_____

_____

_____

2. Think of past hurt that you know God has healed you from today, how is God using your experiences for your own good and/or the good of others?

_____

_____

_____

_____

_____

_____

_____

_____

_____

_____

_____

3. What changes remain for you to complete for a successful mind renewal? Write them down and develop a plan of action to execute this week.

_____

_____

_____

_____

_____

_____

_____

_____

_____

_____

_____

_____

CHAPTER Five

Heal Me

> *The Lord is close to the brokenhearted and saves those who are crushed in spirit.*
> *– Psalm 34:18 NIV*

DISCERN WHERE YOU ARE HURTING AND GET READY FOR GOD TO HEAL YOU

Your closet cleanse and reorganization are underway, but you may be battling all sorts of feelings and emotions. "Oh, but my grandmother gave me that dress and she passed away two years ago." "Those are good solid shoes…yes, they are out of season and not my taste, but I want to keep them." Understand that the new season God is taking you into requires for you to leave what you are clinging to behind and in this moment, that just so happens to be past hurt. Say it aloud, "Heal Me, Lord!"

"Sticks and stones can break

> *If we want God to fix our lives, we must be in a position of prayer. We must also have faith to believe that God will help us, no matter how severe our situations may be.*

my bones, but words will never hurt me." That is the biggest lie I remember reciting as a child. When someone hurts our feelings, or says something that touches our sore spots, wounds re-open because they never fully closed. It is though you were hurt all over again and the feelings are fresh. Sometimes, revisiting that place of pain we experienced during our foundational years, is essential so that we might be propelled into a place of victory. This is difficult, and this can be hard, but if we allow God to perform spiritual open-heart surgery on us, we can become completely healed.

    I was diagnosed with cancer - kidney cancer a few years ago. I found myself numb and unsure of what was going to happen to me. I do not care how saved you are, when you hear that you have cancer, you are going to feel something deep down. There are no symptoms for kidney cancer. 90% of people who have kidney cancer do not know they have it until it reaches stage 4. Now knowing these facts, I realize it was nobody, but God that sent me to the doctor right on time, but my trials did not stop there.

    A few months after recovering, I experienced another attack on my health. I was home alone cooking, and my pressure cooker exploded on me. My body was drenched in 450 degrees hot water. I was traumatized. My husband soon arrived and drove us to Southern Maryland Hospital. I kept screaming because it was so painful. After trying to help me there, eventually they sent me to the burn unit at Washington Hospital Center. Once admitted, a couple of days later I had to go through yet another surgery, I had earlier endured surgery for cancer. They gave me a skin graft. At home my husband had to change my bandages every day. I hated the way I looked. It was just a mess. This is when the depression started, and I discovered I could not heal myself – only God could do that, and He will do the same for you.

A Victor asks God for Healing

Remember when you were a little child, and you or one of your friends would run down the street and someone would fall on the ground? That kid would run home with his or her open, broken-skinned knee. If that skinned knee were untreated, what would happen? The skin would build crust and develop a scab. Once it crusted over, full of blood and dirt because it was not addressed, it would never heal properly. If instead, the child asked for his or her parent's help and that broken skin was treated, it would heal. Suppose the hurt child's parent

> *The process can sting a bit, but God begins to close those open wounds and they heal. Afterwards, we can victoriously walk into living the way God intended for us to live.*

dressed his or her wound and placed a little alcohol or peroxide on it? The wound may sting a bit and that process can be painful. What if the parent took it a step further and rubbed Neosporin on it, and applied a band aid? This is what it is like when we ask God to heal us from our past hurts and pains. The process can sting a bit, but God begins to close those open wounds and they heal. Afterwards, we can victoriously walk into living the way God intended for us to live. God wants to heal all your hurts, issues, and wounds today.

People need healing across the board. No matter your background or vocation, healing is something we all need. This also applies to those of us in ministry. There are people all over the world preaching that have not fully healed. For example, all my insecurities surfaced after the burns. As I was ministering to others, the burns brought to the surface what needed ministering to inside me. It took that horrible accident for me to acknowledge my insecurities birthed from my past. It was then that I finally allowed God to heal me and position me for my purpose in my personal life and ministry! We must go back to the original place of hurt, where our pain lies

> *Begin to talk to God about how mad you are and how you feel about what you went through, and say, "I acknowledge how I feel. Now I need You, God, to heal my hurt." Only God can.*

so that God can heal us. Talk about how you feel. Speak from a place of victory! Eliminate the victimized thoughts of your past. Just as you would in therapy, get it out of your system. Begin to talk to God about how mad you are and how you feel about what you went through, and say," I acknowledge how I feel. Now I need You, God, to heal my hurt." Only God can.

Change your perspective about what you endured in your past, right now. Continue to use the wisdom that God gave you and yes, be vigilant. Walking out of your past into your present testifies to the fact that you are WINNING! Your belief in the realness of God establishes that you already have victory. If you got through it, you survived it, you conquered it, and that means you have purpose. What you went through is so that someone else might overcome by hearing your testimony because you survived it. You did not succumb to your situation. You did not succumb to your circumstances. You did not die in the wilderness of disease, molestation, rape, betrayal, divorce, or rejection. Yes, you were hit, but God healed you and you recovered. Now God is ready to restore! When you are totally healed you operate differently, and look at life through different lens. You cannot erase the past, but you can change your response to the past and God wants to help you accomplish this.

I cannot erase what I have been through and neither can

you, but my response to my past has changed and I encourage you to change yours. It happened. Those things were just a part of your life. You are not a victim. No longer be offended. No. Change your mindset as you learn who you are in Christ. My grandmother would tell me, "Teach people how to treat you." Now I know who I am. Why did it take me so many years, tears, and sleepless nights to get it? I do not know, but now I get it. Everybody has his or her own journey and process.

SOME THINGS, ONLY GOD CAN WASH AWAY

As I endured my healing process, I would not allow my husband to see me uncovered. It had nothing to do with how he treated me. He was very sweet, understanding, and supportive. But, I still felt the way I did. At that point, all my insecurities were on the table. Many of those insecurities were there long before the burns, but the burns brought them to the surface. I found myself deep in depression. That situation weighed heavily on me; I had never experienced depression at that level before.

On Sunday mornings, my face was beat. My hair was slayed. I had it all together from the outside. I did this for a good two-year run. Next, I endured another surgical procedure during the third year post my burn incident. Once you are burned, burn sensations can return at any time because the burns penetrate deep into the nerves. As a result, I was in constant pain. This is what it is like when we allow unresolved pain to linger in our hearts. For me, it was another layer of heaviness weighing me down. I continued to dislike things about myself. I did not like the way I looked. I did not like the way I was feeling. Even though I had a husband who was constantly telling me I was beautiful, I still did not feel beautiful. Then, I became angry with God. I felt empty because I did not understand what God was doing. I was aware "to whom much is given, much is required" (Luke 12:48), but I still thought, "Lord, what in the world? Why would You do this to me?" I was filled with rage, but God finally delivered me, and I am thankful.

I do not look like what I have been through and neither will you, once you submit and yield to God, and receive His healing. No matter what you are going through, always know God is the source of your strength. According to Psalm 61:2, you should say, "…Lead me to the Rock, that is higher than I … when my heart is overwhelmed." God is this rock. God, the Rock, our Heavenly Father, taught me the meaning of His Holy scriptures, and how to wholly lean on Him, especially when I cannot handle what is happening all around me. He will do the same for you.

GOD CAN BIRTH SOMETHING GOOD FROM YOUR TRIALS, IF YOU'LL LET HIM

Our assurance of healing is not in our works, but our belief system. You must believe God at His word. I know without God, I would literally lose my natural mind. I always tell people, when you are at the end of yourself, you are in a good place. Because I embraced a new state of mind, God birthed this book, "Lord, Fix My Life." Just imagine, what God is waiting and eager to birth in your new life! I came to realize that I could not be fixed by my own strength. Your intelligence or amount of degrees you have achieved will not allow you to fix yourself. It takes God, The Healer, to do this. Even if you read a million self-help books, you cannot fix yourself and you cannot heal yourself. You may not know it today, but eventually you will need God.

Personally, God healed me differently that I thought He would. He performed spiritual open-heart surgery and revealed that He allowed hardships and trials to occur in my life, so I could see what was hurting inside. God's surgery changed my life, it really did! My afflictions provided an opportunity for me to better understand God and follow His statutes. Yes, it took all of this for me to truly see *me*. It took the trials for me to understand the person God had created. Through hardships, I came to understand my weaknesses and strengths. My brokenness revealed what I needed to work on and I was able to step back and allow God to do a perfect work. I am reminded of Romans 8:18, "For I consider that the sufferings of this present time are not worth comparing with the glory that is going to be revealed to us." Yes, this lets me know, while it was rough, it was worth it!

Overcomer to Overcomer, you must face it. Like me, you have tried everything you could to fix it, but nothing has worked. For some, you have tried alcohol, drugs, sex, or relationships. For others, you have tried being a workaholic, shopaholic, and over eating or not eating at all. You have tried everything, but in your own strength, you could not fix it. This is great! Trust me because it is often at the end of our capabilities and our intelligence, that we stop fighting and allow God to heal us. Just relax. Give it all to Jesus. God can, and He will heal you today. Only, trust Him.

I am so grateful God stepped in my life when He did. The core of knowing who you are in God can be found through asking God to reveal the purpose of your pain. During my own quest, God revealed who I was and who I was not, equipping me to rebuke the enemy's lies. Think about

> *My brokenness revealed what I needed to work on and I was able to step back and allow God to do a perfect work.*

battles in your own life right now – know, you will conquer every one of those obstacles if you go with God. Recently, I studied the eagle and learned the eagle has a decision to make when it turns 40 years old. It must decide whether it will die or go through 150 days of re-creation. I thought about this and mirrored it to the human experience. Like the eagle, we must all go through our process, and during the process, we can choose to die in our painful situations, or we can choose to soar. I pray you will choose the latter.

Complete the exercise below to apply what you have been reading so far:

1) What is hindering you from making an appointment with God for your spiritual open-heart surgery? Journal about these hindrances.

_____

_____

_____

_____

_____

_____

_____

_____

2) Just the thought of getting prepared for a healing process is painful because it will inevitably re-open your wounds. What takeaways have you learned from reading this chapter that will push you towards your healing anyway?

_____

_____

_____

_____

_____

_____

_____

_____

_____

_____

3) You are at a place where you must decide, like the eagle. What strategies can you put in place so that you will soar?

CHAPTER Six

Know Your Enemy

> *Be alert and of sober mind. Your enemy the devil prowls around like a roaring lion looking for someone to devour. Resist him, standing firm in the faith, because you know that the family of believers throughout the world is undergoing the same kind of sufferings. And the God of all grace, who called you to his eternal glory in Christ, after you have suffered a little while, will himself restore you and make you strong, firm and steadfast. To him be the power for ever and ever. Amen.*
> *- 1 Peter 5:8-11 NIV*

Sometimes disorder becomes normal to us because we have been blinded by the enemy for so long. It becomes a way of life. You may toss your socks in a pile to the left corner of your closet. In that pile there are other articles of clothing intertwined. All the while, you know your socks belong inside your dresser drawer. Despite your ability to locate your socks eventually, you are losing minutes rummaging through a

> *Sometimes disorder becomes normal to us because we have been blinded by the enemy for so long.*

disorganized pile of clothes to find them every day. Minutes turn into hours, hours turn into days, and so forth. Armed with the ability to discern the enemy's tactics, you will see more clearly as God begins to lift the scales from your eyes. God wants you to walk into a lifestyle of order, a system where you may simply retrieve your socks from the dresser drawer to the right. Just imagine how you will go through your new morning routine with ease, and enjoy the time you have reclaimed!

Your enemy, Satan, is a time snatcher also known as a time thief. Satan's ultimate goal is to steal your voice and keep you from completing your purpose that God created you to fulfill in the earth. Satan approaches you according to your spiritual level of faith and where you are in the process of completing the various tasks God has assigned to you. If you are new to following Christ, know that problems persist even after developing a relationship with God. I have come to notice that Satan attacks us most before we initiate the thing that God has called to do. For example, whenever people decide to get married, all hell breaks loose beforehand. This is important as we know that marriage symbolizes Christ's love for the church, the people of God. Another example, if God has called you to create something

> *Your enemy, Satan, is a time snatcher also known as a time thief.*

new, Satan will attack your mind, your tools, etc. in efforts to keep you from starting. The reason being it is far easier to stop someone before he or she begins because once you begin you know that you can do it and you have the gumption to persevere beyond the attacks. So, Satan tries to invite you to participate in a knockout, dragged out fight beforehand.

Pay attention, God always sends help because the battle is not yours. See Exodus 14:14, "The Lord will fight for you; you need only to be still." You will receive encouragement in the form of personal visions and prophecies. These visions may come in the form of dreams. Prophecies may come from people you know and do not know. God does this to provide you with the strength to endure and keep going towards, what is for you, new and unchartered territory.

Understand Satan's levels of approach. When we are young, we are trained to fear Satan and his evil ways like a big boogie monster on television. Once you dispel that myth, Satan changes his approach and uses different devices. He will begin to attack your body or your loved ones; then, when you persevere beyond those things he uses distractions. Distractions are fine-tuned as he becomes clever in ascertaining your stumbling blocks or weak points overtime. For example, he may start with attacking a relationship that was going well, it could be a business or friendly relationship. You and the other individual are agreeable and effective at working together, and then suddenly and out of nowhere the other person has a complete change in attitude. They demonstrate a huge personality shift where they begin to act irrationally and behave in ways that are unwarranted and inappropriate. Once you survive this, the distractions shift into a form you are less likely to recognize.

Satan will present opportunities that may seem like good things on the surface, but they are not God things. God things, meaning what God created specifically for you to do, according to His will for your life. Overtime, as you become closer to God and begin to study purpose, this will begin to make more sense. If you fall into this trap, Satan will have accomplished his goal of taking you away from your specific purpose.

I could provide many examples, but the most immediate one would be the struggles I faced writing this chapter. While attacks have come throughout the duration of writing this book, working on this chapter was different. Specifically, when I sat down to write, *Know Your Enemy,* I faced more distractions than I had at any other point. I did not immediately recognize it though. I felt fatigued. I was bothered by pain in my body. Everyone was vying for my attention. I wanted to take a break and recreation was calling me - something as simple as watching television. You see, the enemy is cunning; this attack was subtle, yet very distracting.

Remember, Satan does not want you to know your power. Satan also does not want you to be able to harness your power effectively. Satan wants to remain as that mysterious figure – the boogie man from your childhood and the one whom you try to downplay or pretend does not exist during adulthood. Yes, he is sneaky, but if you take the time to study God's Word and come to know who Satan is, your enemy; you will be able to surpass the obstacles and stumbling blocks that he will toss onto your path. Pray and ask God to help you. I assure you this will work to your benefit. You may be thinking, "How?" Understand that Romans 8:28 is still at work, "And we know that in all things God works for the good of those who love him, who[a] have been called according to his purpose." God's Word says, "ALL THINGS," and God cannot lie. Numbers 23:19 says, "God is not human, that he should lie, not a human being, that he should change his mind. Does he speak and then not act? Does he promise and not fulfill?" The good most likely will not be evident as you hurdle the obstacles and endure Satan's attacks, but it will be revealed following. Sometimes, we are blessed to see the reason after the attack subsides, and there are other rare occasions when we understand that God will provide revelation when we meet Him in Heaven. Just trust God.

You will become more victorious once you understand the adversary. Without this knowledge, the enemy will play on your weaknesses and vulnerabilities. He will victimize, mislead, and confuse you with deception. Understand and identify his schemes. Do not allow him to grab a foothold (any part) in your mind or play with your emotions. Think about our focus scripture for this chapter, 1 Peter 5:8-12; Satan is an expert at what he does, but equipped with the right knowledge, you will become more powerful to withstand his attacks as the Holy Spirit fights for you.

As you grow closer to God and gain a better understanding of spiritual warfare, you will soon be able to boast in the face of trials. 2 Corinthians 12:9 says, "But he said to me, 'My grace is sufficient for you, for my power is made perfect in weakness.' Therefore I will boast all the more gladly about my weaknesses, so that Christ's power may rest on me." Furthermore, when you feel weak, as though the weight of the world is resting on your shoulders, remind yourself of Ephesians 6:12, "Our struggle is not against flesh and blood, but against the spiritual forces of evil in the heavenly realms". This scripture advises that we are not fighting with humans but

> *You will become more victorious once you understand the adversary.*

spiritual forces of evil. To allow God to fix your life, you must recognize and be aware of all tactics discussed throughout this chapter and more. Below is an itemization of some of Satan's methods expanded.

1. Deception: Satan is an expert at exaggerating things to make them seem worse than what they are. The key to recognizing the enemy's deceptive tactics is to inspect the thoughts you are having and compare them to the Word of God. Ask yourself, "Is this thought biblical?" "Is this thought focused on what is 'true, noble, and pure' according to Phil 4:8?" If not, quickly reject it from your mind understanding it did not come from God. Most importantly, remember God is always in control in any situation.

2. Fear: We are told to fear nothing nor anyone in many scriptures throughout the Bible. God's Word reminds us repeatedly, that we do not have to be afraid. Contrarily, the enemy wants us to be bogged down with worry and fear. If left unaddressed, fear can paralyze you, as it is the opposite of faith. Sometimes we can fear failure, success, or the unknown. It is in these times that we must remember 2 Timothy 1:7 "For God has not given us a spirit of fear and timidity, but of power, love, and self-discipline."

3. Discouragement: The enemy desires to influence your thoughts in a way to make you believe that you are incapable of living well and fulfilling God's will for your life. His job is to discourage you and push you towards a place of depression. Remember God is our Creator and God is a way maker! He will always see you through your trials, no matter how hard or impossible they may seem to conquer. Satan also likes to persuade us into thinking we are not equipped for what God has called us to do. He is a liar and as the father of liars, the enemy is incapable of telling the truth. Overcome discouragement with faith in God, joy, and love! Don't allow this dream destroyer to hinder or delay your dreams any longer!

4. Distraction: The enemy distracts in efforts to delay and cause stagnation of your purpose. Satan works tirelessly to draw the children of God away from God's will. Have you ever noticed that whenever you decide to read God's Word or go to church something always come up? There are always interruptions. Some are very subtle. Remember the Word of God in 1 Corinthians 10:13 says, "No temptation has overtaken you that is not common to man. God is faithful, and he will not let you be tempted beyond your ability, but with the temptation he will also provide the way of escape, that you may be able to endure it." With this awareness, know that you are strong enough to endure the distractions. God allowed them to happen, and the occurrence of them is evidence of this notion.

5. Rejection: God will never reject you. Satan wants to emphasize the moments that you have felt rejected in your life. Yes, you will encounter people who do not like you from time to time, but remember you are not alone in this. This scripture referring to Jesus says, "If the world hates you, know that it has hated me before it hated you" (John 15:18). Sometimes we find ourselves jumping through hoops to please people to avoid rejection. Unfortunately, this behavior is conditioned by the people in our lives who only seem to love us based on performance. If you do what they expect you to do or give what they expect you to give to them, then they accept you. That is why we must understand the beauty of God's unconditional love. He loves us when we do and when we don't follow His plan. God loves and accepts us always, even in our weakness and even in our mess. Rejection is an emotional prison the enemy uses to keep us in the bondage of condemnation, guilt, people-pleasing, and fear. Fight through with the power of God and allow God to teach you true love.

Your enemy, Satan, brings condemnation. The enemy brings guilt and does not want you to move forward. Resist and keep going. The enemy recognizes how blessed you are, and he is doing everything in his power to make you doubt your Savior, the God you serve. This is not the end of you. This is not the end of your life. Take the new equipment that God has provided to you and start over again. Be refreshed, be restored, and be renewed. Your God is far greater and more powerful than the enemy can ever be! Be strong and go forward with God.

Complete the exercise below to apply what you have been reading so far:

1) Identify three things in your life that you know with certainty God has called you to complete that you have delayed. Now determine the tactics the enemy has used to cause this stagnation. Evaluate and assess them so that you may better recognize them in the future. It is time to execute!

_____

_____

_____

_____

_____

_____

_____

_____

2) This week initiate a plan and execute what you have been putting off. Vow to take breaks and rest as needed, but get right back up to resume your work until completed. When the enemy rears his ugly head, pray and deal with it accordingly, but it is important that you immediately jump back into what God has called you to do as soon as you are able.

3) What lies have Satan replayed in your mind repeatedly? After you identify them, reject them and rebuke Satan accordingly as many times as necessary.

_____

_____

_____

_____

_____

_____

_____

4) Recall the foundation of your thoughts on faith and figure out how this foundation has impacted your faith in God today. Write this down in a prayer journal.

5) Pray and ask God to eliminate anything that is a hindrance to your faith growing in Him daily.

6) What are some ways that you can promote further processing and development of your faith?

_____

_____

_____

_____

_____

_____

_____

_____

Eliminate the Baggage of Unforgiveness

> *"Come to me, all you who are weary and burdened, and I will give you rest. Take my yoke upon you and learn from me, for I am gentle and humble in heart, and you will find rest for your souls. For my yoke is easy and my burden is light." - Matthew 11:28-30(NIV)*

YES, UNFORGIVENESS IS BAGGAGE AND FORGIVENESS ELIMINATES IT

You must get rid of some things and it is okay. You have already identified your closet as jam-packed. Hoarding can become a way of life to the point that we do not recognize we have been holding onto garbage, camouflaged baggage, that is weighing us down. There are some super oversized tattered pants in your closet. There are also significantly undersized dresses with rips down the seams and it is time to throw them all away. Dump out all the old baggage.

We need to be able to forgive. Unforgiveness forces an unnecessary weight upon us because we believe we have a

> *When you forgive, you are not forgiving the offense, but you are freeing yourself.*

right to remain angry. When you forgive, you are not forgiving the offense, but you are freeing yourself. When you hold onto unforgiveness, it can actually bring sickness into your physical body. It limits you and restrains you. You cannot truly have balance and joy if you are dwelling there. It is a choice, and not a right to not forgive. You do not have a right to not forgive. Imagine, the person you are harboring resentment against is sleeping peacefully at night, while you are awake holding onto unforgiveness.

When you forgive you find joy and peace. Forgiving is not synonymous with forgotten. As the analogy suggests, you cannot un-ring a bell, but you can change how you perceived the sound the bell made when it rung. Forgiveness is for you so that you can move forward. If you avoid this process, you will soon find the cousins of unforgiveness entering your heart. These close relatives are known as bitterness, strife, and rage. Protect your peace and release the pain of your past through forgiveness. Remember, it is important to forgive because God first, forgave us.

It's one of the greatest gifts you can give yourself, to forgive. Forgive everybody. ~ Maya Angelou

PEOPLE CAN ALSO BE BAGGAGE:

To totally allow God to fix our lives we must learn to distance ourselves from things or people that weigh us down. Every connection is not a God connection. Check your circle of friends and associates and ascertain the following:

1) Do they exemplify where you are going?
2) Are they still doing things that you are trying to get delivered from?
3) Do they tell you what you can't do while offering no support for what you should do instead?
4) Are they successful or productive?
5) Do they get jealous when you are successful?
6) Are they against the changes God has made in you?
7) Do they always bring up bad things from your past and refuse to see the good God is doing in your life?

If you have answered, "yes" to any of these questions then those people are hindering your progress and eventually you will find yourself back in the sunken place of your past. Continue to love them, but do not allow their negative conversation and mentality cause you to doubt what God is doing in your life. Don't let someone who gave up on his or her dreams talk you out of going after yours.

BAGGAGE SLOWS YOU DOWN

It is very important for you to have open communication with God during this season of elimination and letting things and/or people go. For it is during this season that God speaks. Baggage not only makes us heavy, it slows us down because it is packed with the spirit of delay which produces a spirit of procrastination or slowness. Slowness causes us to look and behave awkwardly and operate in a posture that is bent over. This remind me of a great biblical story of the woman who was bent over for 18 years in Luke 13:10-17 (NIV):

> On a Sabbath Jesus was teaching in one of the synagogues, and a woman was there who had been crippled by a spirit for eighteen years. She was bent over and could not straighten up at all. When Jesus saw her, he called her forward and said to her, "Woman, you are set free from your infirmity." Then he put his hands on her, and immediately she straightened up and praised God. Indignant because Jesus had healed on the Sabbath, the synagogue leader said to the people, "There are six days for work. So come and be healed on those days, not on

the Sabbath." The Lord answered him, "You hypocrites! Doesn't each of you on the Sabbath untie your ox or donkey from the stall and lead it out to give it water? Then should not this woman, a daughter of Abraham, whom Satan has kept bound for eighteen long years, be set free on the Sabbath day from what bound her?" When he said this, all his opponents were humiliated, but the people were delighted with all the wonderful things he was doing.

This woman referenced in Luke was broken down. She was broken down and looked at the ground for 18 long years of her life. When I think about this woman in a modern context, I imagine her going to the prom looking at the ground. That is if she had the confidence to go to the prom at all. She had to groom herself looking at the ground. She went to the grocery store looking at the ground. She did everything while looking down at the ground. The Bible says, "Lift up your heads, you gates; be lifted up, you ancient doors, that the King of glory may come in" (Psalm 24:7 NIV). The King of Glory can't come in until you lift your head up. And this woman couldn't lift her head until she came into God's house, the synagogue. She came, looking down, and operating in all that baggage. She carried this weight all the way to the balcony because women were required to sit there during this period. The Lord looked over everyone else and up to the balcony and said, "Woman, you come here," and when she came, it brought glory to God! First, be reminded, the Lord has not forgotten about you. Just as he did not forget about this woman; he looked past all those people and pointed her out! He touched her and said, "Woman, thou art loosed from your infirmity." It was her faith that healed her. It was her faith that changed her mind. It was her faith that changed her situation. Will you allow your FAITH to change your situation through forgiveness?

Tear Down the Walls

We carry many bags unnecessarily. The bags of stress, pride, frustration, and offenses. Much of our baggage is weighing us down because we haven't dealt with it. It remains unresolved. We have all established walls of defense in efforts to protect ourselves from feeling the pain we have not addressed. You may remember the mentioning of my own walls in a previous chapter. We make excuses and say things such as, "Oh I was born like this. This is just who I am." These notions are not true. Situations and experiences have made us the way we are. Even though we tried to brush it all under the rug, the residue is still there.

We must identify what will eliminate the baggage, remove the scales, and the layers of hurt. We must initiate the demolition of the walls we have built over time. Our walls have been fortified and re-painted over, and over again. We tell ourselves, "Oh, this looks good, I'll just cover it up with this. Oh, that looks good, I'll just cover it up with that." We continuously mask our feelings, but our hurt remains untouched. This is evident because as soon as someone touches an area that has hurt us before, it re-activates and begins to hurt all over again. This occurs because we haven't yet healed properly. When you are properly healed you can see the person that previously hurt you and be unbothered and not affected. Only God possesses the right sized bulldozer to tear down the walls and the structures you have erected providing a false sense of protection around your heart. If you allow God to perform reconstruction, you can successfully move forward being fastened securely to Him and redeemed by the blood of the lamb that was slain for all our sins, Jesus Christ.

BE REAL WITH GOD, TELL HIM HOW YOU FEEL

God wants to know how you feel. Our God knows all, but He's also saying, "Acknowledge Me in all your ways and I shall direct your paths" (Proverbs 3:6). He just wants to hear it, He wants you to get it out of your system. That is the way God operates. He wants us to share it with Him, so that we may release it over to Him. When we fully give it over to God, He can remove the old baggage.

The Bible tells us, "...old things have passed away..." (2 Corinthians 5:17). This verse should serve as your reminder to not wallow in the past. God has given you the power to rebuke the enemy when he replays in your mind those situations that caused hurt and pain in your life. When you forgive, you can kick Satan out because he no longer possesses an *unforgiveness* hold over you. Forgiveness plays a major role in letting go of the past. We can't let go unless we forgive.

For example, if I hadn't taken time out with God to work on forgiveness and letting go before I met my husband, then Pastor Limes would have paid for the hurt I was holding onto from my previous relationships. With that old baggage within my grasp, I would have never trusted or loved again. I would have just been a *Mad Black Woman*! Pastor Limes would have borne the weight of all that junk. I am thankful that God unpacked those bags and healed my wounds before sending my husband to me. Because I eliminated my old

> *He wants us to share it with Him, so that we may release it over to Him.*

baggage, I reached a turning point for the better. It is amazing what God can do when we allow Him to eliminate the baggage of unforgiveness from our lives! Let God help you unpack today. There is no excuse good enough to not allow God to do it. Trust me, you are worth it.

Complete the exercise below to apply what you have been reading so far:

1) If you are struggling with identifying the baggage of unforgiveness in your life, take a moment to think about what triggers you emotionally in your relationships. Jot this down, as this can provide clues to where your baggage lies.

_____

_____

_____

_____

_____

_____

_____

_____

2) Ask yourself the following questions:

    a. When I look in my bags what names do I see that should be released through forgiveness?

_____

_____

    b. Who have I yet to forgive?

_____

_____

    c. What names still cause me to roll my eyes and sigh deep breaths whenever I hear or read them?

_____

_____

    d. What else am I holding onto that I haven't really dealt with yet?

_____

_____

e. What incidents have I brushed under the rug that have left residue behind?

_____

_____

3) Tell God what's holding you back from truly trusting Him with getting rid of the baggage in your life.

_____

_____

_____

_____

_____

_____

_____

_____

Find Your Happy Place!

> *I am not saying this because I am in need, for I have learned to be content whatever the circumstances.*
> *– Phil 4:11 NIV*

*T*ake a deep breath! Inhale the fresh aroma that is now flowing through your closet. You have cleaned your closet and now it is time to embrace your new life and find your happy place. In this chapter you will learn how to discover what makes you happy with Jesus as the center of your joy! Perhaps you have been in survival mode for so long that you have lost sight of it. If this happens to be you, it is time to get to know your new self and identify what brings you happiness. God desires for you to walk into the fresh and bright new season that is upon you this very moment!

Let Nothing Rob Your Happiness!

Gratitude is the core of happiness. Learn to be grateful. Learn

Discover healthy ways to be happy. to count your blessings. Make it a daily practice. Just as sure as you are living, you will experience trials – as we have established previously, but you must always remember that happiness is a choice and it is up to you to protect it. No matter the intentions of external forces, always remember that you can choose to be happy and you can choose to have joy. A great way to put these concepts into practice is through understanding that every season is purposeful - good and bad. Now that you know this, it is time to move forward. Discover healthy ways to be happy. Learn to have fun! Remember, God has shifted you into your new season of happiness and you must protect it along with your new state of mind and overall peace. Now you are free, and it is important that you protect your space. Practice daily self-care.

Learn what brings you happiness by finding out what activities appeal to your interest. Could it be exercising? Physical fitness is a proven method to aid in happiness because exercise releases endorphins and endorphins generate happy feelings. Rest and activity go hand and hand. Balance is key. When I find myself overwhelmed with too many things to do, tired, and unbalanced; I realize I am being robbed of my happiness. So, I had to learn how to slow down and how to prioritize. I also learned the importance of "me" time. Even if it is just walking through the mall or buying a brand new tube of lipstick!

> So, I had to learn how to slow down and how to prioritize. I also learned the importance of "me" time.

As you become more active in pursuit of positivity, remember to not over do it. Make it a habit to be around positive people and practice positive speech. Do what brings you joy that is good for your overall well-being and your body! How about sports? Do you enjoy attending sporting events? Are you interested in bowling? How about golfing or playing board games? Some are into dancing and others are into music. Whatever your thing is, do it and enjoy yourself always remembering to balance it with work and rest!

When your mind thinks of your past, reflect on the good it has brought you. Look around you, God has stepped into your life and He has blessed you. This is another great place to interject counting your blessings! Keep moving forward. Remember, "Therefore, if anyone is in Christ, the new creation has come:[a] The old has gone, the new is here!" (2 Cor 5:17 NIV). Another part of finding your happy place involves aligning your desires with God's desires for your life. Pray and ask God what He desires and wills for you. Ask God to reveal these things to you with clarity and without distractions so that you will see and understand what He says. Also ask God to prepare your heart, mind, and spirit to receive the plans He has for your life and you be ready to shift accordingly. As you move forward in God; progress, grow, and learn to love yourself. Resist the temptation to compare yourself to anyone, always embracing yourself as the unique masterpiece God designed!

Your feelings are important. Listen to them, but do not be ruled by them. Understand that you have the power to focus in a positive direction. See your value. Know your self-worth and be confident in who God has created you to be. Intentionally, avoid negativity. No one knows you better than you know yourself. Take note of the things that make you happy versus the things that you find negative. Avoid, those negative things.
Know you were created to WIN! Embrace this concept right now.
God uses experiences and if we pay attention, He can use one specific situation to reveal who He has created us to be. Whatever call God has placed on your life, I can assure you that He wants you to win. He wants you to be victorious! He wants you to be successful. He wants you to achieve every goal, aspiration, priority, and dream you have in your life!

Avoid, those negative things.

Reflect daily, think about the victories you have already conquered and what God has allowed you to successfully come through. Remind yourself that in the same way God has blessed you to overcome, He will also bless you through whatever will come in your future. Your job is to stay in the light. Look at the people who depend on you and find joy in serving, especially on difficult days. Remember it is up to you to find your happy place and dwell there! As you work to navigate this new terrain, it is my hope and prayer that the list below will be helpful:

TOP 10 HIT LIST FOR HAPPINESS

1. Love God
2. Love yourself
3. Practice gratitude daily
4. Smile
5. Exercise regularly and eat healthy
6. Remain in the company of positive people
7. Have regular "Me" time
8. Learn to say no
9. Learn new skills & seek wisdom always
10. No comparisons

Complete the exercise below to apply what you have been reading so far:

1) Identify what is robbing you of your happiness today and declare that it will no more. Determine a list of decrees and declarations for yourself to find your happiness and embrace it.

_____

_____

_____

_____

_____

_____

_____

_____

_____

2) Do you tend to complain or count the negatives in your life? If so, challenge yourself to create a gratitude journal. At the end of each night for the next seven days write down at least five things that you are grateful for in that journal. Five represents grace and it is my prayer that God will grant you the grace you need to get through this journey.

3) Are there any people in your life who are interrupting your happiness? If so, determine, if these are relationships that you should keep or let go. If you opt to keep them, develop a plan to compartmentalize your interactions with these people to protect your peace.

_____

_____

_____

_____

_____

_____

_____

CHAPTER Nine

Clean Out Your Closet

> *Search me, God, and know my heart; test me and know my anxious thoughts. See if there is any offensive way in me, and lead me in the way everlasting.*
> *- Psalm 139:23-24 NIV*

Congratulations you have successfully reached the final chapter of *Lord Fix My Life!* Now, you are aware of the importance of having faith in God and that your words and prayers are powerful. You also know the value of renewing your mind and you have learned the importance of asking God for healing. With awareness of who the true enemy is, you have been armed with the necessary tools to get rid of old baggage. Finally, as you embrace your happiness; Now, you can freely release the victim mindset from your former days and embrace the victor that God has placed within!

All these tools are integral to having a clean closet, a clean slate for your new way of life. The focus scripture for this chapter calls us to make a bold and courageous request of God.

> And when God examines, He never leaves you the same.

Let's begin our conclusion to this book so that you can commence application of what you've learned, here.

When we say, "Search me, God," we are literally, presenting ourselves to God for thorough examination. And when God examines, He never leaves you the same. God restores. God builds you up to a place that will be better than what you perceived to be your best self, before. It is instrumental for your personal growth that you ask God to clean out your closet if you truly want God to fix your life. "Search me, God" equals "Lord, Fix My Life."

Understand, it is only God that can truly mend the broken areas that lie within you. Your complete and total healing lies in being delivered from unforgiveness, bitterness, and rejection. Take another look at the closet on the front cover of this book. I can guarantee that much of the clutter that needs to be eliminated from your closet is hinged upon the above-mentioned areas. Choose to forgive. Release your bitterness. No longer bear the burdens you have packed into your closet due to past rejection. God accepted you before you were placed in your mother's womb. Let Go and Let God.

Meditate on Psalm 139:13-17 NIV.

For you created my inmost being;
you knit me together in my mother's womb.
I praise you because I am fearfully and wonderfully made;
your works are wonderful,
I know that full well.
My frame was not hidden from you
when I was made in the secret place,
when I was woven together in the depths of the earth.
Your eyes saw my unformed body;
all the days ordained for me were written in your book
before one of them came to be.
How precious to me are your thoughts,[a] God!

This scripture testifies to how your very existence and your being here on earth is demonstrative of God's good feelings about your life. This text lets us know that God's thoughts towards you reach far beyond acceptance. For God was your Creator. God loves you so much that He had the audacity to plan out all your days on this earth before He placed you inside your mother's womb. Now that we know this, tuck this away for recall the next time the enemy tempts you to have a rejection pity party with him.

LET GO OF EMOTIONAL HOARDING, LET GOD HELP YOU

Emotional hoarding is something that must be eliminated. Your clean closet is attainable, but you must begin the work to receive the manifestation that you seek. *Let go.* Don't allow resentment to turn into bitterness because you haven't yet, let God heal your heart. *Let God.* I know that I had to let go of resentment in my own life from previous relationships and experiences. If I had not, my ministry would be in jeopardy – or there may not have been a ministry for me at all. I had to let God heal me so that I could learn how to love my husband properly. Without God, free will could have ruined the possibility of my marriage to Pastor Limes, altogether.

Remember, never allow Satan to gradually dump trash into the backyard of your life ever again. When you see him carrying a plate (a negative thought) stop him right in the street. Don't even allow him to come into your driveway. Do this by learning to rebuke and reject the adversary daily. Ask God to increase your discernment. When God begins to show you the hearts of people you are surrounded by in your life, believe Him and act accordingly the first time. Believe what God reveals – good and bad. Don't stick your head in the sand hoping that bad things will fix themselves or that bad people will go away on their own. Many times, they will not.

We've also discussed the importance of learning who is Judas versus John in your life. *Let go and let God* applies to distancing yourself from harmful things, habits, and people alike. This can be difficult for people of faith to employ sometimes because somewhere we have aligned "being a Christian" with "being a doormat" and God never wants us to be a doormat for anyone. As Believers, we were made to be courageous – which is why we are victorious! Always remember that God will never call you to endure an abusive situation. God's love for you commands a higher standard. Love yourself enough to choose to operate in God's plan, which is the best plan, for your life.

OUT WITH THE OLD, IN WITH THE NEW!

Let's face it. Many of our closets are overflowing with clutter because we have the tendency to hold onto things we do not need. Some of these things may not seem obviously bad, at first glance. As a matter of fact, there are some things that may have been good for us in another season that no longer fit us because of our new lifestyles. Imagine, trying to squeeze a three-year old into clothing sized for a newborn. Yes, it's ridiculous. Remember this whenever you are tempted to squeeze back into a position that was sized for an old season of your life. Unfortunately, old things continue to utilize space that should be reserved for new things (habits) that are useful for your present and future seasons, until you decide to release them.

There are several things that we do not like, but keep anyway, as some sort of memento from the past to remind us of a former time. Think about that family heirloom you have, maybe it's a piece of furniture that sticks out like a sore thumb that your grandmother passed down to you from her grandmother. You think it's hideous, but there's a greater problem, it's taking up space. Imagine in that same space instead, greater room and a smaller piece of furniture that suits your taste. Now, wasn't that refreshing! It can be this very same way once you remove the painful memories from your mind that have inhibited you from fully embracing the *happy* of your present. Then, you will be able to walk into the bright future that God has in store for you.

It's true, we internalize things. We have the tendency to never discuss certain issues and therefore, we never get them out of our systems. I propose a different approach. Find a way to express your thoughts and feelings. You can begin by journaling. Some find it therapeutic to journal to God, specifically. It may feel odd at first, but it will drive you to become more conscious about truly casting your cares onto Jesus. You may also desire to speak to someone trustworthy, that has proven themselves to be your confidant, and if it applies; know that professional counseling and spiritual direction are wonderful options to consider. As a matter of fact, it can help you reconcile thoughts that you have tucked away, simply by hearing yourself say them aloud.

Growing up I, too, had a habit of internalizing my feelings because I didn't think I could share them with anyone. I learned when you internalize things, they can eat away at you like cancer. They can metastasize in great magnitudes and become worse than what they were originally. First, you may have been troubled by worry and fear; and now you are plagued by the threat of resentment becoming bitterness and bitterness turning into hatred. Let it all go. However, you choose to release the excess garbage from your closet, you must, so that you can begin the rest of your life with a fresh perspective.

NO MORE RESOLUTIONS – STICK WITH IT

Now it's time to move forward. And while you will resolve and vow to do many things during your lifetime, it is important to remember that the words you write down and say from your mouth will only manifest once you begin to act with your brain, hands, and feet. James 2: 14-17 NIV reads:

> *I learned when you internalize things, they can eat away at you like cancer.*

What good is it, my brothers and sisters, if someone claims to have faith but has no deeds? Can such faith save them? Suppose a brother or a sister is without clothes and daily food. If one of you says to them, "Go in peace; keep warm and well fed," but does nothing about their physical needs, what good is it? In the same way, faith by itself, if it is not accompanied by action, is dead.

Without action, the journey you've taken along with me by reading this book will be moot. Don't allow this to be a set of wasted minutes of your life because you are not willing to apply what you have learned. Act, today! A great start will be to complete the *Reflections* located at the end of each chapter throughout this book.

Set your life's goals and stick to them. Now imagine your closet clean. It's neat, it is organized, and it even gives off a sweet aroma! Because you will have been removing many things, you will have now made room for the new that God desires to give you. Make room for the new perspective that you have imagined. Move forward in God. He's waiting. Look forward to the bright new future ahead simply because you've asked, "Lord Fix My Life!"

> *He wants us to share it with Him, so that we may release it over to Him.*

Complete the exercise below to apply what you have been reading so far:

1) If you haven't yet began writing in your journal, now is the time to do so. Begin to write down your exact feelings. Release them to God. Make it a habit to release so that you won't be tempted to internalize your feelings instead.

_____

_____

_____

_____

_____

_____

_____

_____

2) Have you been writing down and saying your declarations based on your new perspective so far? If yes, great! If no, let's start today! Challenge yourself to recite one declaration at the top of each morning following your morning prayers.

_____

_____

_____

_____

_____

_____

_____

_____

_____

_____

_____

3) There is a stigma in some cultures against seeking professional counsel. If this has been your experience, and you desire counseling, challenge yourself to locate a counselor and schedule an appointment this week. If for some reason you don't have a good experience and your personalities are able to work together, give it at least two more attempts. If your personalities are a mismatch, do not give up on counseling. Search for another counselor and try again as soon as possible.

ABOUT THE *Author*

Rev. Michelle Denise Limes, a native of Washington, D.C., is the proud wife of Pastor R. Sean Limes, mother of their three children, Marcus, Ashlee, and Aaron, and grandmother to Maya. Pastor and Co-Pastor Limes serve The City of David Ministries in Forestville, MD, under the leadership of Bishop Glen A. Staples, Th.D., D.Min, D.D., Senior Pastor and Presiding Prelate of the Temple of Praise International Fellowship of Churches, Inc. Co-Pastor Limes studied at Maple Springs Bible College and was licensed to minister in May 2001. This was followed by her ordination in October 2004. She is currently pursuing a degree in Psychology. God has placed a mantle of anointing on Limes to preach and teach the gospel in a relatable way that resonates with the masses.

Limes is the CEO and Founder of *iamConfidence*, an organization created to support participants to *confidently* be who God has called them to be in the earth. This movement was designed to ignite confidence and self-worth in individuals to propel them into their Kingdom purposes within every area of their lives. Through programmatic workshops and worship services, iamConfidence participants receive social skills development, along with counseling and restorative sessions to aid in recovery from traumatic experiences.

Additionally, Co-Pastor Limes is the owner Agape Enrichment Childcare and Imagine Summer Program for the Arts. Limes, an overcomer and mother to many in her community, and has an extensive background of service. She has served in various capacities in church. She has facilitated youth ministry, choir direction, worship leading, women's ministry, and marriage ministry. As her background suggests, she is willing and ready to operate in any assignment that God releases her to serve within. Limes also enjoys collaboration with others in ministry. One event she is proud of, Behind the Makeup, not only provided an opportunity for her to join forces with other women in ministry, but it also provided a vehicle to address issues that women cope with in silence, like depression. Limes has worked within the nonprofit sector for twenty years and has also worked FEMA under the f Department of Homeland Security. Limes stands on Psalm 91:1 (NIV), "Whoever dwells in the shelter of the Most High will rest in the shadow of the Almighty." This scripture exemplifies her understanding that we must all lean and depend on God for everything. Furthermore, she believes that with God as the source of your strength, you may rediscover, redeem, and reignite your dreams, goals, and God-given purpose as God reveals to you, who you are!

www.ingramcontent.com/pod-product-compliance
Lightning Source LLC
Chambersburg PA
CBHW070456100426
42743CB00010B/1639